T0065289

Raiva 108

Spiritual Vibrations

Taresh Dass Nahar

authorHOUSE®

AuthorHouse™ UK
1663 Liberty Drive
Bloomington, IN 47403 USA
www.authorhouse.co.uk
Phone: 0800.197.4150

© 2015 Taresh Dass Nahar. All rights reserved.

No part of this book may be reproduced, stored in a retrieval system, or transmitted by any means without the written permission of the author.

Published by AuthorHouse 01/25/2016

ISBN: 978-1-5049-3731-3 (sc)
ISBN: 978-1-5049-3730-6 (hc)
ISBN: 978-1-5049-3732-0 (e)

Print information available on the last page.

Any people depicted in stock imagery provided by Thinkstock are models, and such images are being used for illustrative purposes only. Certain stock imagery © Thinkstock.

This book is printed on acid-free paper.

Because of the dynamic nature of the Internet, any web addresses or links contained in this book may have changed since publication and may no longer be valid. The views expressed in this work are solely those of the author and do not necessarily reflect the views of the publisher, and the publisher hereby disclaims any responsibility for them.

Raiva Series

My Guru

Hazoor Syed Peer Ishfaq Mohi-U-Dhin Shah Sahib has greatly helped me to broaden my awareness of Self Realisation. Gurji has truly opened my mind beyond religious boundaries and dogmatic ritualistic practice.

<u>My Beloved Parents</u>

This book is dedicated to my deceased parents. My father Veero Dass and mother Dhano Dass.

My parents did not go to school, their main aim in life was to give their children a good education.

My father Veero Dass passed away January 1992 at the age of 72 years and my mother Dhano Dass passed away August 1973 at the age of 44 years.

Author

Taresh Dass Nahar

My background has its roots deep in Sanatan Dharma and Sufism. My ancestors from the Valmiki community adopted Sufism, as they had been deprived of their human rights by the distorted teachings of Hinduism, in the form of the cast system.

I am proud, that my parents did not let go of Hinduism. The scriptures of Hinduism have nothing to do with the distortion of their teachings.

Meera,

It had been many years since i last saw my uncle Taresh, we had much to catch up on and he told me about the poetry book he was working on. I know him to be an amazing songwriter as well as a poet, and being a songwriter myself i was most interested in uncle Taresh's works.

I had the privilege of proof reading this body of work. I was blown away! Each poem is written with such passion and insight. Some poems are very thought provoking. I would describe this work as "food for the soul".

I have recently released my debut single " We Collide" which is now available for download on iTunes and all other digital outlets. The video is also featured on Youtube and Vevo, with over 10,000 views in it's first few weeks of release. My uncle Taresh has been very supportive of me and my music.

Uncle Taresh has kindly allowed me to include the links for my music (social media) below.

I am extremely proud of him and his achievements not only as a songwriter, but as a poet too. I really hope you all enjoy this work of art as much as i did.

www.facebook.com/meeraHQ
www.twitter.com/meerastar1
www.instagram.com/meeramusic

subscribe to the official channel - MeeraVevo

Light, Love and Peace
Meera Gharu

Hans Raj,

I met up with Taresh after many years, we have always had a spiritual connection. As soon as we met we got into a conversation about Sanathan Dharma, spirituality and Baghwan Valmik Ji. The conversation was most enlightening, it was wonderful to meet someone like minded.

After a few meetings Taresh mentioned his forth coming book of poems and asked me to proof read for him. I was most surprised and elated, although I was a little apprehensive at first. I had not read much poetry prior to this. However, I accepted Taresh's request and i am glad i did.

Reading Taresh's book was very thought provoking and took me on a very special spiritual journey. I hope anyone who takes the time to read this magnificent piece of work enjoys it as much as I did.

Love, peace and best wishes :-
Hans Raj Gharu

Iain Stewart

Taresh Nahar is more than a poet. He is a sage, philosopher and theologian rolled into one. The world often divides itself along religious and non-religious lines.

Taresh through his poetry calls on people to forget the little differences and celebrate what we have in common. To think in an increasingly secular and materialistic world of where real lasting satisfaction and fulfilment can be found. His poetry reminds us that at the heart of every faith there is great wisdom and a desire to serve God. Not through worship alone for that can become empty unless it is combined with the compassionate acts of helping others.

General Secretary Edinburgh Interfaith Association, MA Interreligious Relations

Ramesh Lal Mattu:-
Seeker of Truth

"Taresh's poetry touches my heart and soul. No doubt it is very deep in parts and just skimming will not bring the credit it deserves. It is thought provoking and transcends the mere worldly existence. I recommend it completely."

Paramjit Singh Basi

"I have known Taresh Nahar almost for twenty years. His ideology is based on equality and justice He has been a staunch supporter of the under privilege class of our society and he can feel the pulse of masses. He has seen lots of ups and down in life and he has been a victim himself of feudalistic arrogance.

He is a good human being and I wish him well for his contribution to society."

<u>*Acknowledgement*</u>

Without the help support and encouragement of certain people in my life this publication would not have been possible.

First of all I would like to acknowledge my Guru Syed Peer Ishfaq Mohi-U-Dhin Shah Sahib 108, who is my spiritual mentor and guide in all walks of life.

Krishan Marwaha a close friend and a brotherly figure was the first person to inspire me to compile my work in book form.

Manjulika Singh and myself present Sanatan Dharam Chaupal on AwazFM 107.2 every Saturday Morning 8-9am. Manjulika has always appreciated my poetry and encouraged me to keep focused on my spiritual path and supported me with the completion of Raiva 108 Anmol Moti, as well as Raiva 108 Spiritual Vibrations.

Ramesh Lal Mattu has inspired and encouraged me on my spiritual journey and discouraged me from worldly attachment. Ramesh plays a very important role model in my life.

Warris Abdullah a good friend and a presenter on Awaz FM, has helped and guided me in all walks of life. His contribution has been greatly appreciated.

All my brothers deserve a special mention in me being what I am today, good bad or ugly they have all influenced me in some way.

A special mention goes to brothers Doc Prem and Ramesh. Ramesh peacefully passed away Jan 1st 2009. He is dearly missed every day.

Javed Sattar Founding Director of AwazFM has always been on standby, whenever I have needed any technical support in the broadcasting studio or advice in the compilation of Spiritual

Vibrations and my last book Anmol Moti. His support and help has always been of great value.

Mrs Adarsh Khullar Chairperson and founder of Ektha a single womens support group for her sisterly support guidance and faith in me.

A heartily thanks to my son Ravinder and my daughter-in-law Seema and of course my grandsons Aryan and Ashwin.

Kiran and my heavenly granddaughter Maya are all very special to me.

A special thanks to Iain Stewart, Meera Gharu and Hans Raj Gharu for proof reading this manuscript and making suggestions which were greatly appreciated.

Finally I am greatly thankful to the most important person in my life, my wife Rekha Ji for putting up with me and supporting me when all others failed.

Contents Page One

Contents Page Two

Who

Who am I to say Who is good and who is bad
Why judge others The mad and the sad

Forgive my sins In the darkness of my heart
When I look into myself And the deeds of my past

I am no better Than others I say
My ego is big And it gets in my way

Why hide sins Then point still at others
My badness within My innocent face covers

Cleanse the soul With meditation and good deeds
The inner light Will destroy my greed

Who am I to say Who is good and who is bad
Why judge others The mad and the sad

Poem 1

We are never in a position to judge others, as we never really know all the facts. In the worldly sense, we are judging all the time and it is important to judge.

Mixing and interacting with the right people is very important. We need to protect our self's and the health and safety of our family and friends.

We are not responsible for everything and everybody. But on a spiritual note we need to take responsibility for all we can, within our limitations.

Loving

Loving you are You have goodness within
Righteous you are The Word lives within

Greatful you are You have compassion within
Caring you are Love always wins

Good karmic deeds Is the light within
Your righteous path Will lead you to him

You serve the Lord Without an expectation
You love the Lord Without any frustration

You are in the father The infinity of creation
You are made with love The path of salvation

Loving you are You have goodness within
Righteous you are The Word lives within

Poem 2

Loving caring and sharing is very important. Being conscious of the laws of nature and how our actions and other people's actions affect the self and all else in creation, is also very important.

Man is the highest of all living beings born in the spiritual image of God. He is the master and has superiority over all on earth.

All of creation is the body of the creator. Everything on earth has been created for a purpose, to support all life through its evolutionary stage on earth.

The purpose of life is to thank the creator for all experiences given to us. To show our thanks we must walk the path of righteousness as taught by a spiritual master. This path leads us to ultimate happiness and bliss. Our final abode with our heavenly father, beyond the limitations of our own consciousness.

Marriage

Marriage is love Marriage is divine
Marriage is sacred It's your life and mine

Marriage is doing Things together
Marriage is supporting And trusting the other

Love is for all The heart is for one
Marriage is forever And you are the one

Whatever is mine Is also yours
Your pain is mine And mines is yours

Marriage is forgiving When things go wrong
Living for God and Singing love songs

Marriage is the righteous Path of God
The world evolves With the will of the lord

The battle is tough Our egos are strong
If you do not surrender Marriage goes wrong

Our bodies are two The soul is one
You are the light And I am the sun

Marriage is love Marriage is divine
Marriage is sacred It's your life and mine

Poem 3

The most important relation between any two beings is of trust and respect. This type of relationship is called friendship. Beyond friendship is love, ideally we should love everybody.

The nature of humans in the worldly sense is that we all need company, help and support on our journey through life and vice versa. People of opposite sex have a great attraction for each other. This type of loving bond between man and women in most cases leads to a marital relationship. The institution of marriage has been blessed by God and passed onto mankind through prophets and scriptures.

A loving marital relationship between man and women is a very special one. Only man and women can have a physical relationship, which keeps the evolution of life in circulation.

My Love

You are my love You are my life
You are my Jesus You are my Christ

Where ever I look It is you I see
You are in the birds You are in the bees

You are in the skies And beyond my eyes
Within my heart Where the sun never dies

You were always there For me every where
You are in the dark In the sins of my heart

One day I will see The light that is me
When my soul is clean It shines in me

You are my love You are my life
You are my Jesus You are my Christ

Poem 4

Our goal and purpose in life is to realise through our worldly experiences, there is no true love between mortal human beings. Only highly evolved spiritual people can give true love. Spiritual masters have true love for everyone, yet have no attachment.

True love is bliss. Only bliss can give an individual eternal satisfaction. Jesus the son of God, and as the human manifestation of God, could give us that, "true love".

True love has no boundaries and no limits of time speed and distance. The consciousness of highly evolved spiritual master's can be anywhere. They have the spiritual power to manifest in whatever form and in whatever time period they wish. The word of spiritual master's, is the word of God.

Wisdom

Words of wisdom Are nice to know
Words of wisdom When life is low

Words of wisdom To love every day
Words of wisdom That show the way

Words of wisdom Where maturity flows
Words of wisdom That righteousness knows

Words of wisdom They live in the heart
Words of wisdom Are the Light in the dark

The greatest words Are words of love
The greatest love Is the love for love

The greatest thoughts Are in meditation
The soul is the wave God is the ocean

Words of wisdom Are nice to know
Words of wisdom When life is low

Poem 5

Wisdom guides an individual onto the path of righteousness. The path of righteousness sucks an individual into divine love. Ethics and morals that promote harmony peace and prosperity in family community and country, the nation and the rest of the world are all components of divine love.

Love is the gist of all religions. Unconditional love can only be practised by people who have no attachment to material wealth and worldly way's.

Journey

Life is a journey We have to play the game
The body is the vehicle Our destination is the same

Love is light Darkness never reigns
All religions are different God has many names

Our reason to be born Is to seek out the Lord
The kingdom of heaven That resides in us all

God is within We are all in the father
Word are the thoughts The thoughts of the father

Creation is the will The will of the Lord
Nothing was ever born Without the Word of God

Life is a journey You have to play the game
The body is the vehicle Our destination is the same

Poem 6

God has given us life for a purpose. The purpose of life is self realisation. What we think we are, we are not. The world we think is real, is only a dream. We cannot ignore this dream, as through this dream we all evolve to a higher stage of spiritual elevation. Each one of us has to take his journey on his own, our destination is the same. Finally with the help and guidance of a spiritual master, we all merge into the infinite ocean of Super Consciousness.

The world was created by the creator as a, "Universal Evolutionary Learning University of Life", for all. We must monitor, access and evaluate ourselves, then make the relevant changes and move on.

We must believe in God (Divine Love) and surrender to his divine manifestation, as a spiritual master. He then blesses us with worldly and spiritual knowledge and guides us onto of the path of his righteousness. The practice of love, care and service are all components of self realisation. Divine Light is a consciousness that has no boundaries of time, distance, past, present and future. Divine Love, has total control.

No Wings

I live with the clouds I fly with the winds
I flow with the rivers And the stars with no wings

I am in the animals In the plants I live
In and out Of all particles I exist

I was never born I will never die
I need no food I will always survive

No heat I need I fear no cold
I hate no one For I am their soul

I do no bad I can never be sad
I have no wish No desire to be rich

No attachment I have To material things
Nothing in creation Will forever sing

I fear no one Only what I have done
The laws of karma Applies to everyone

I am in the father And the father is in me
This I will experience When there is no me

Poem 7

The Super Soul (Divine Consciousness) is present all the time, everywhere in the past the present and the future.

At the highest stage of spiritual elevation the soul has achieved total purification. It can now merge with the Super Soul to be one with our Heavenly Father.

Karma are the laws of nature that regulate goodness and badness, to ensure balance harmony and justice.

Aum

Aum are vibrations The thoughtron's of God
Ishwar the creator Manifests in them all

Creation is the body The body of God
There are no boundaries Neither has the Lord

Light is divine The reality of all
It lives beyond The mind of us all

Bav sagar is a fire The plane of realization
Clean up your mind To reach your destination

With righteous deeds We can never go wrong
You give us your strength Your love is so strong

To get your love Love all of creation
The bad and the ugly Are only imagination

Aum are vibrations The thoughtrons of God
Ishwar the creator Manifests in them all

Poem 8

Aum in Hinduism is exactly the same as the "Word", as in the bible. Everything comes from the Word and hence everything comes from Aum. For anything to materialise, initially it has to exist as a thought. The Word can be said to be infinite thoughtrons of God. Thoughtrons are the thoughts of God.

Creation is infinite God exists in all of creation, everywhere at the same time. Hence it can be said that all of creation is the body of God. To love God we have to love everything in creation.

Ishwar is a name given to God in Hinduism, it means the one and only creator and controller. Divine Light is the reality of all, Divine Light is God. Out of Divine Light manifests the, "Word". All of creation in Hinduism is referred to as Bav Sagar meaning, the "Ocean of Illusion".

Only man has the potential to realise through the path of righteousness, prayer and meditation, the scriptures and the guidance of a spiritual master that all of creation is just a dream of the mind.

Light

I search for a light Within my heart
Deep into my mind Beyond all thoughts

My heart is a cage It has no door
The mind is a bird It stays no more

My thoughts are good Not always wrong
The bird of the mind Has a will of it's own

It flies around With a mind so strong
When I pull it back It cries and it moans

My control of the self Is very very weak
The will of my mind Has too many leaks

My weaknesses are strong My intentions go on
The more I pray Nothing ever goes wrong

I see the light It comes and it goes
I focus within From the heart it flows

I search for a light Within my heart
Deep into my mind Beyond all thoughts

Poem 9

During meditation we need to be totally focused. If we talk or have any thoughts, we cut God communication out of our consciousness. It is very difficult to still the mind, as it flies around with a will of its own.

The more we meditate the easier it becomes. The mind can be compared to a bird in a cage that has no door. The bird goes in and out of the cage as it wishes, but if we keep on catching it and putting it back into the cage, eventually it gets used to the idea that there is no escape, and stops even trying.

The deeper we go into meditation and calm the storm of the mind, the closer we get to "Divine light".

Just Pray

Pray to God Who gives us light
Pray to the Lord Who shines so bright

Pray to unite The world with love
Unity and diversity Respect is a must

Religions were born To praise the Lord
In the house of God Only purity calls

Pray for love That lives within
Love all people And forgive their sins

Pray for all Help those in need
Pray for the goodness That everyone needs

Help them all The good and the bad
Pray for joy When we are sad

Keep still and focus Your mind within
Love them all Love always wins

Pray to God Who gives us light
Pray to the Lord Who shines so bright

Poem 10

The more we pray and meditate the more our consciousness expands, the more spiritually enlightened we become. Being intuitive and forgiving are some of the qualities of a spiritual person. Walking the path of righteousness becomes easier.

Although all religions praise the Lord, there are many differences in our religious personalities. Respecting each other and not letting our religious differences get in the way of love, unity, peace, prosperity and harmony is very important. Being good to all and helping your neighbours is of prime importance.

Forgiveness

Happy new day All year on And all life long
Look after the bad And the wicked and the sad

Forgive their wrongs And forgive your sins
Never hold a grudge And cleanse within

No conditions for forgiveness Nor for love
Only love to love When you get no love

No tit nor tat For the sake of love
With love in your heart Expect no love

Look after the rest God does his best
The laws of nature Will never ever rest

The world evolves As time moves on
Universal disasters Goodness goes wrong

No pilgrim nor money Can save your skin
No friends no rituals When one does sins

Suppress your ego And control your desires
Surrender to the self Your inner fire

Happy new day All year on And all life long
Look after the bad And the wicked and the sad

Poem 11

If we cannot forgive others, God will not forgive us. Forgiveness should have no conditions. In the spiritual sense, we should love everyone. Yet have no expectation that they will love us back.

We must help everyone and do good deeds. If you have faith, then God will look after your needs. When anyone does wrong, the laws of nature take control to regulate justice.

Reading a scripture or ritualistic practice will not get us out of trouble once one have committed a sin or done wrong to someone. We must directly approach that individual for forgiveness.

One must in the true sense repent and surrender to the righteous way of living. Only then will God forgive you. Eternal happiness can only be achieved by living a life of purity free of sin and serving those in need.

Beauty

Beauty is within Beauty is the soul
Beauty is the light That beauty only knows

Beauty is love Without a desire
Beauty is God A cosy fire

Beautiful are you You are so good
A good clean heart And healthy good looks

Beauty I look Within your deeds
Beauty I look Within your speech

Your are so simple You shine within
You are the light That lives within

Beauty is within Beauty is the soul
Beauty is the light That beauty only knows

Beautifully enlightened souls are very conscious that they don't do anything wrong. They are very tolerant and loving towards everyone, they do not judge or get angry or have any expectations from anyone. Always content with what they have and yet they work very hard. God loves the fact that they have surrendered to righteousness and looks after all their needs.

An uncontaminated soul is a clean soul, beauty contentment and happiness at its best. A soul's spiritual consciousness is affected by its experiences, its thoughts and the condition of its physical body. A healthy mind and body can focus better on the consciousness deep within.

Purpose

What is the purpose Of life on this earth
If born to die And the end of the self

Do good to others That suffer my friend
Blessings from them Will help you in the end

Material wealth Will stay on this earth
Except the talent And the skills in yourself

Karma my friends Effects us all
Yours and mines Righteousness calls

Why be greedy And deprive someone else
Of food and drink So he dies in hell

Heaven is earth And Hell also too
Some have billions Only luxury will do

What is the purpose Of life on earth
If born to die And the end of the self

Poem 13

Is there any point in living if when we die, we come to an end. There must be a reason why we are expected to do good, there must be a purpose to life.

By the wisdom of God, the laws of nature have given some people so much wealth that it sticks to them like a disease. Others have worked very hard in devious ways to accumulate their wealth yet, they are still very miserable. Many people have very little food and water and poor health. Everyone lives in their own heaven and hell or somewhere in between. Heaven and hell are both a state of individual emotional consciousness based on our experiences of the past and the present.

Responsibility we have to help and serve those in need. Freedom we have to do what we want. Again and again we have been reminded by prophets and wise men that we should be walking the path of righteousness. God will not force us to do anything. He wants us to use our free will, to suppress our ego and surrender to His will.

Our consciousness will then merge into the Super Consciousness of our Heavenly father to be one with Him, our purpose and final destination.

Pray

Pray for peace We need your love
Pray to God Who is never ever bad

Pray for truth The light within
Convince yourself You will always win

Pray for unity Forgive all sins
Pray in the self Heaven is within

Pray for the sick The rich and the poor
Never be too smart And never be a fool

Pray for the world Love all of creation
Control your ego Have loving emotions

Pray for peace We need your love
Pray to God Who is never ever bad

Poem 14

Being mortal human beings, at times we are unaware of the consequences of our actions. Our experiences of emotional and physical pain and mental stress make us wonder.

Eventually through our evolutionary experiences of life, we realise that nobody or nothing on this material plane can give us the everlasting pleasure we would like to have. Hence, we turn our focus for help to a creator. A consciousness of super power, control and ultimate ability which scriptures believe has made the heavens and the earth and everything within.

When we lose hope, we surrender to this reality which is beyond our perception and logic and call to it for help. God listens when we have faith, if we genuinely repent.

The more spiritually inclined people ask for forgiveness, enlightenment and happiness for all people, good or bad and the sick and the sad.

Love

I got plenty of love From my father and mother
And ethics and morals To help one another

They looked after me My material needs
They gave me food And cut off my weeds

They prepared me for My life to come
Gave me the tools So that life could be won

When they were gone I lost my path
I could not see Because of the dark

I met good friends Who came and went
They gave me the love That always ends

Very few are here Still with me
Sometimes my family Stands by me

The infinity of love Lives within
True love for God Is the only thing

I need the love That believes in me
I need the love That walks by me

I need that love When I am wrong
I need that love I am not very strong

I need that love Forever and ever
I need a Guru To love me for ever

I found a Guru Who could give me the light
The infinity of love That is always bright

All he wants Is love from me
All he needs Is goodness in me

All he wants is Faith and trust
For all his love A clean heart is a must

I got plenty of love From my father and mother
And ethics and morals To help one another

Poem 15

A soul which has attachment to this physical world in anyway, is one that has not reached its final goal of life when it was on this earthly plane. As a result, this soul has to take birth again. It takes birth according to its karmic account.

Generally speaking most good parents give their children love, ethics, morals and education and other skills that would prepare them for their lives ahead.

As we progress through life parents eventually pass on. Friends come and go. When there is no proper loving relationship for guidance, it is very easy for one to lose his/her path, in this journey of life. At this stage in one's life, a spiritual mentor is of great importance to focus one's attention on worldly and spiritual aims.

A clean heart that is lovingly conscious of the creator always has peace harmony and happiness. The individual purified soul eventually reaches the door of salvation through which it merges within the Super Soul.

A Guru is a spiritual mentor who advises and guides his disciples on their worldly righteous duties, as well as spiritual self realisation.

Battle

I look into my heart To see a light
That shines in the dark When karma is bright

In the darkness of thoughts I see the evil in me
Which hides the spark That shines in me

My storm of consciousness Is difficult to calm
When I control my senses I improve my chance

My mind is weak My focus is low
The weaknesses of the mind Say ho ho

My fight is tough My loses are high
My breaths of life Say bye bye

I lose the fight To surrender myself
My ego is strong I damage myself

I love the world That holds me back
The material things I think I lack

I lose the fight Each and every day
I lose my life And go away one day

God is good He never forgets
I do something wrong I always regret

Another life He gives I get another chance
To enter the battle And spiritually advance

Each and very day The battle goes on
I forget the battle But time moves on

I look into my heart To see a light
That shines in the dark When karma is bright

Poem 16

During meditation I try to focus within my consciousness, deep beyond my thoughts. What I see depends on my focus and karmic account. Thoughts of wrong deeds and other good or bad experiences or desires and senses of the body, block out the, "Divine Light".

I need to have determination ie a strong will power to continue the fight. The battle is tough. My invaluable breaths are my greatest lose. Every second this battle has to be fought. When I see the light, it comes and it goes. My experiences in meditation give me the strength to fight on. They are a catalyst, on my path of righteousness bliss and eternal happiness.

One lifetime is not enough to totally purify the soul and qualify it for salvation. God is so loving and caring that he gives us many chances, to try again and again. He loves us and wants us back home to our heavenly kingdom.

Time

When our time is over We all must go
When the body falls off We must let go

The pleasures of the world Get in our way
Our friends and family Have to stay

They cry for us They think we die
We also cry And say bye bye

They cannot listen They cannot see
Tears in our eyes Our emotional cries

Ash has no wish Light has no voice
The soul goes on Into the father it belongs

Please let me go There is no choice
I have to follow My karmic voice

When our time is over We all have to go
When the body falls off We must let go

Poem 17

The only thing guaranteed in life is death. We all have to move on according to the laws of nature. The soul is so accustomed to the physical body, it get's emotionally very distressed when it has to leave the body.

Unfinished work, attachment to people and accumulated wealth make it very difficult for the soul to move onto its next evolutionary stage.

Close family and friends are very disturbed when we die. For various reasons some selfish some not, they cry to express their loose.

It takes time for the soul to realise that life was just a dream. Eventually and very quickly it realises that it is impossible for it to get back into that dream. The soul is so attached to the characters and events of its dream, it emotionally cries. Those that are left behind cannot see the soul crying and reaching out to them, but the soul can see them.

When the soul sees his family and friends cry, it finds it difficult to move on according to the laws of karma, as defined by the Super Soul. Karma are our good and bad deeds.

Lessons

Life has many Lessons to teach
A tough life Is what I got

Life gives many Kicks in the teeth
Teeth I have lost A lot

Life can be rough Plenty of bad luck
Hard work can achieve A lot

Actions for peace Do good deeds
Prayer will help you A lot

Battles will come Many still to be won
Surrender only To the Lord my son

Life has many Lessons to teach
A tough life Is what I got

Life gives many Kicks in the teeth
Teeth I have lost A lot

Poem 18

Throughout our lives we learn many lessons. No one really has it easy. Though some have it much easier than others and some have it extremely difficult. In our own way, we all go through our own heaven and hell.

Hard work is very important. Lady luck helps those that work hard. Good loving caring actions for others and prayer make it much easier to face the bad times in life. There will be many battles in life that still have to be fought, we must fight on. We should only surrender to righteousness. Then leave the rest to the laws of nature.

My Soul

My heart is on fire Your light is my desire
You live in my heart We can never be apart

When I am down Your are by my side
When my life is dark You give me your light

When I am weak You lift me up
You give me the strength That picks me up

The immortal light That lives in me
The soul of my soul I cannot see

You talk to me When I prey alone
You walk with me When things go wrong

My heart is on fire Your love is my desire
You live in my heart We can never be apart

Poem 19

The soul is a wave of consciousness from the infinite ocean of the consciousness of the Super Soul. There is always a direct contact between the soul and the Super Soul.

The Super Soul has no limitations. The soul has limitations of the body and feels its dependence on the physical plane, which cause it to forget its true identity.

It looks for happiness through its experiences and the senses of the physical body and realises that the reality of life is duality (happiness and sorrow) and that nothing lasts forever. Everything is born to die. This results in further confusion and sorrow.

Eventually as the soul evolves, it realises that the only way to permanent happiness is to take the path of righteousness. The path of righteousness can only be taken with belief in a true spiritual master, as our mentor and guide. On this path we face many difficulties. Eventually this path takes us deep into our unlimited consciousness, as one with our heavenly father.

Duality

Everything in life Has a duality my friend
Happiness and sorrow We suffer to the end

Scriptures we need Spiritual masters too
To show us the path That leads us to you

Deep in our consciousness The light within
The path of goodness Will lead you to him

Seek Him within Stay calm and cool
No movement at all You will never be a fool

Dharmic karma Is the will of the Lord
Surrender my friend Have love for them all

Everything in life Has a duality my friend
Happiness and sorrow We suffer to the end

Poem 20

Duality is the reality of life in the worldly sense. Everything fluctuates from one extreme to the other nothing remains the same. Sometimes there is pain sometimes there is pleasure. Sometimes there is happiness and sometimes sorrow. Some things are true and some all false. In this worldly state of duality we suffer, due to the misuse of our free will.

Once one has totally surrendered to the will of the Lord, only then he qualifies for Anand otherwise known as Bliss. When soul conscious is one with the consciousness of the Super Soul, there is no duality. If you deviate from the path of righteousness, you lose the consciousness of Bliss.

Enemies

Why have enemies And wars to be won
Peace and harmony And life could be fun

Education and jobs And dignity for all
Stand up for equality Let no one fall

The rich and the poor Are not all the same
Respect them both Don't reject the lame

Love is cool No hatred at all
All colours of man God loves them all

The good and the bad Please help them all
Only love will reign And the devil will fall

Why have enemies And wars to be won
Peace and harmony And life could be fun

Poem 21

If we are free of ego and good at caring and sharing and respect each other's differences of culture, religion and personalities. Then there would be no reason for confrontations. We would all have the potential to lead a peaceful and a harmonious life.

If we are fair to all, the good and the bad and everyone get's the same opportunities and necessities of education and jobs, housing and food. Then there is no reason why we cannot have unity and prosperity for all.

On the other hand we have to be content in whatever situation we find ourselves in. At the same time we must work hard and pray to God to help us remove our sufferings and the pains of others.

A clean heart has a loving caring and sharing attitude to all. It has no hatred, or any negativity of tit for tat. It always wants to be good.

All Life

Happy new day All year on And all life long
Look after the bad The wicked And the sad

Look after the rest And pass every test
The laws of nature Are the righteous best

The world evolves As goodness moves on
Universal disasters As badness gets strong

Look after the family Nothing should go wrong
Give up your ego And sing a loving song

No lies nor money Can save your skin
Be good to all So everybody wins

Surrender to goodness Control your desires
Look into yourself Your inner fire

Expect no return Nothing material may come
In the spiritual sense You must love everyone

Happy new day All year on And all life long
Look after the bad The wicked And the sad

Poem 22

Every day of one's life should be celebrated, not just a birthday or festive season. Every day we should help those in need, without judging them. When looking after other people, don't worry about yourself. God will take good care of all your needs. We must have faith.

When goodness and justice is practised, peace harmony and prosperity eventually shine. When badness takes control, disasters are not far away.

When things go wrong one has to look into his/her egoistic attitudes. One cannot buy himself out of trouble with money and lies. The Universal laws of Nature cannot be bought out, by ritualistic practice.

When being good to others don't expect any return in the material sense, it may not come. Your efforts will be rewarded, and you will get a return from the spiritual world in some way or other.

Prayer

I Pray for my brothers My sisters and friends
And I pray for all Who drive me round the bend

God bless you all With health and wealth
May God support you With his love himself

His wisdom and his blessings Shine over all
The rich and the poor The small and the tall

The good and the bad Get harmony and peace
Salvation through righteousness His love is so deep

I pray for my brothers My sisters and friends
And I pray for all Who drive me round the bend

Poem 23

Good righteous actions of serving caring and sharing, truth and justice are all qualities of a Godly person. Prayer and meditation are very important. In meditation sit still and focus to remove your inner barrier of thoughts, in order to open out your consciousness to the consciousness of the Super Soul.

In prayer one should ask the Super Soul to bless and remove the sufferings of all relatives good or bad. And all friends and foes as well as all other people, that one does not know.

Pretty Face

Your pretty face Makes everyone smile
The magic in your eyes Puts my heart on fire

Your slim dark looks Is heaven above
You live within In my heart with love

Take good care And always be strong
Look after your health Never ever go wrong

Love is eternal True love never dies
Love can laugh It can also cry

Without your love I will surely die
If I have your blessings I will always fly

Your pretty face Makes everyone smile
The magic in your eyes Puts my heart on fire

Poem 24

If you have a good loving relationship with someone you will find them very pretty. Sincere true love is not easy to find. Only God in his human manifestation (prophets) can give pure unselfish love.

When you love someone very dearly they are always with you, in your heart and memory. You would advise them to look after themselves and not to stay away for too long.

True love is said to be blind. Anything said by the one you love cannot be wrong. When you are madly in love and miss someone, you may feel sensations of funny pain which can make the heart cry.

Within

There is no evidence Of what God has said
There is no scripture That ignorance has not read

Man is full off Light within
When your will is weak Ego wins

Nothing is born That remains the same
Everything changes Even God's name

What we experience Is only a dream
The only reality That we have seen

Consciousness expands The more we understand
When we still our mind Our thoughts move on

We a need a Guru To inspire us along
We need to persist When things go wrong

The journey is tough The mind is weak
We lack determination When focus we seek

There is no evidence Of what God has said
There is no scripture That ignorance has not read

Poem 25

There are many religions and many divisions in each religion, how can we take religion seriously. For me reality is my own experiences not what I am told. Scriptures cannot help me assess my experiences in life and meditation. Only an enlightened spiritual master can do that.

Everything exists because of our consciousness and the five senses of our physical body. All knowledge comes from within our own consciousness, which expands the more we meditate or pray. Divine Consciousness has no limits.

The past is a dream. The future has still to be dreamt. The present is changing so fast it is not permanent and get's swallowed up, very fast by the cycle of time. Future is an illusion. It vanishes just as quickly through the reality of the present into the darkness of the past.

The journey of life is not easy. We easily lose determination and focus when our mind is weak.

Walk

Walk on his righteousness Walk on his path
Live for others With love in your heart

Be one with a Guru No doubt in your heart
Accept what comes Never be too smart

Happiness is always A pleasure to have
Sadness is a weakness It can make you mad

The light of God Bliss is within
No mandir nor maschid Will trap him within

No scripture can describe Your joys of bliss
No guru or prophet Can give you this wish

The self is the saviour The path is within
The body is a vehicle Love always wins

Live for others To cleanse the self
Surrender yourself Don't remain in your hell

Poem 26

Righteousness are the universal and eternal laws of Divine Love that lead us to our heavenly home. Our consciousness merges into the consciousness of God. The Divine Light of God is shear Bliss.

When we love someone they end up loving us back. If we love a true spiritual master and surrender to him/her we get true love back. Only a spiritual master can give you true love. A guru is a spiritual master.

No religion or scripture has sole rights over salvation.

Today

Today is the day I must have fun
For you are my father And I am your son

Today I will bury My gremlins within
And fight the devil That lives within

Today I will forgive My friends and foes
Love them forever No blame I will show

Today I will live My life to the full
Do my duties The wonder of your will

This could be the last Breadth of my life
To repent my sins And take your advice

Nothing to gain If my ego reigns
I will lose the fight If I remain the same

God is love Love only wants love
Surrender to Love To show that you love

Today is the day I must have fun
For you are my father And I am your son

Poem 27

Life's experiences and wisdom through scriptures make us aware, that God is the father and mother of all creation. The Lord was with us before we were born and will always be with us after we die.

Once we realise this and have faith, life can be great fun, as we journey through life helping and serving those in need.

We are lost in this world and need someone to lead us through this journey to Divine Love. Only one who has made this journey can take us through this spiritual journey. We have to surrender, to one who has walked this path of righteousness and knows our heavenly father.

Ideally we have to love serve and help everyone. We need to have our gremlins well under control. Our gremlins are our habits and desires. We need to forgive those that may have wronged us. This journey has to be taken very seriously and we need to make it as soon as possible. As this breath could be the last breadth of this life.

Chess

Life is a journey A game of chess
Have no emotions If you want to be the best

We need to have desires And aims in life
Realistic aims But always be precise

Without expectations We cannot progress
Family and relatives Never are the best

Hard work good intentions Must always flow
Harmony and peace Where ever you go

Life is a journey A game of chess
Have no emotions If you want to be the best

Poem 28

The journey of life can be compared to a game of chess and snakes and ladders. We have to be very careful and considerate as to how we play this game. To survive in this world, expectations and aims are very important, but they must to be very realistic.

Emotions we cannot avoid, but they have to be well controlled as emotional decisions can get us into trouble. If we have too much attachment to the material world, we could suffer. Nothing is guaranteed in life, except death.

Most people we know, family relatives and others, very rarely measure up to our expectations, unless they have something to gain. Not many people will do something for you without any frustration or expectation. Such friends are very rare and difficult to find.

We must work very hard and have good intentions towards happiness, harmony, peace, prosperity and unity all the time, wherever we go.

Super Soul

The sound barrier And the speed of light
Cannot trap The source and it's might

Fire and water Have no effect
As divine love Is the immortal best

Material elements Have no other source
Everything in creation Our Super Soul controls

All of creation Is made for a purpose
To support all life That is born on it's surface

Man is the King The King of this earth
Everything was made As his drinking well

The sound barrier And the speed of light
Cannot trap The source and it's might

Poem 29

Everything has been created and is controlled by Divine Light, which in the worldly sense is referred to as God. Divine Light is omnipresent, omniconscious and omnipotent. All of creation will dissolve back into its source with time. The cycle of creation will repeat itself.

Everything is made for a purpose. The purpose is to support man through his evolutionary journey to self realisation, through purification of the soul.

Only on the physical plane through righteous actions, with the help of a spiritual master can we progress to purification. Once the soul purification process is completed, the soul then merges with the Super Soul as a drop of water becomes one with the infinite ocean.

Need

I need to have respect And love for others
I need to forgive The mistakes of others

I need to know Who are my friends
I must also know How to befriend

I need to help Those in need
Strength I need To pick up the meek

I need to be happy Make everyone laugh
Especially myself The sick and the sad

The anger within Me must die
Fairness within Should never ever lie

Ego and ignorance Should never ever rule
Wisdom within And always be cool

Heart and the mind Is the house of the soul
Your love and comfort Is my ultimate goal

Poem 30

The path of righteousness is love and peace, caring and sharing and respect for all, as well as helping serving and forgiving others. Anger and ego hold no importance on the spiritual path, being fair to all is a must.

One needs to be sincere and needs to know who his faithful friends are. A spiritual caring personality easily makes friends. The heart and the mind are the home of "Divine Love". Our ultimate goal is to be engulfed, with the loving bliss of our heavenly father.

Blessings

Give me your blessings Give me will power
To suppress my gremlins And kill them for ever

Show me the light The source of creation
Show me the self That is beyond imagination

Infinite love The ocean of bliss
It lives in the heart But never ever ticks

Vibrations of love Divine Light of us all
Unstruck sound That lives in us all

Please oh God The source of all
Beyond the mind And the senses of all

Give me the wisdom The wisdom for all
Actions of goodness In the benefit of all

Infinity of love The soul in us all
Show me your light The reality of all

Poem 31

Blessings from a guru and inner strength we need to walk the path of righteousness. We try to be good, but we need to be super good. Total control we need of our senses, the mind and our consciousness.

Worldly material attractions and our so called earthly loving relationships suck us deep into the clutches of illusion, in religious terms known as the devil. We know we will die one day and that the body will be recycled into the earth. Through lack of awareness determination and will power, we fail to prepare the soul to move onto its next evolutionary stage.

Divine Light and Divine Love are the ultimate experiences of peace and happiness, spiritually known as bliss. They can only be experienced when the mind body and soul are totally in tune with the spiritual vibrations of the Word and Aum, both being the same.

Why

Why do I love This world so much
It gives me pain And love so much

Nothing is permanent It all moves on
Attachment to material Will always go wrong

Worldly things They come and they go
From the earth they come To the earth they flow

The soul from God Into the body it falls
One day it will leave Have no fear at all

Learn to be good And be good to them all
When your mind is clean Satan will fall

Life is a journey For the small and the tall
The roads are tough But the father calls

Focus within Into the light you will win
Prayer and meditation Ultimate peace is within

Poem 32

Soul consciousness gets attached to the physical body and the worldly environment, causing it to suffer at the thought of dying. Through lack of spiritual awareness, we forget that nothing is permanent. Everything is changing. The body eventually falls off and is recycled back into the earth. Eventually the soul will have no choice, but to move onto a different dimension.

In this University of life the nature of man is to appreciate and practice righteousness. Actions of love and goodness is holding the whole universe in a state of stability, harmony, peace, prosperity and unity together.

The consciousness of the mind travels through many dark and dangerous jungles, to face and overcome many beasts within the jungle of the mind. The battle is tough, but it has to be fought. The war is to purify the soul through meditation and good deeds, and eventually merge our consciousness into the Super Consciousness of our Heavenly Father.

Vibrations

You give me vibrations That cleanse my soul
You gave me the love That I only know

You are in my heart And one with me
The righteous path You never leave me

You are not only one Infinity are you
All forms are yours No confusion in you

You comfort my soul When I am down
You hold me up When the world steps down

I am a drop A wave from your ocean
When my soul is pure I am the ocean

You are in my heart The soul of my soul
You are the light That darkness holds

You give me vibrations That cleanse my soul
You gave me the love That I only know

Poem 33

Super Conscious is God, what we call "Divine Light and Divine Love" In totality it is one, in our dream state of life it has infinite forms.

Our consciousness is a finite part of that God's Super Consciousness. The difference being, our soul consciousness is trapped in a physical body and has attachment to the earthly plane. If the body is not kept tuned within its tolerances of health and emotional feelings it suffers, so does the soul.

The Soul can be said to be a wave of the eternal infinite ocean of Super Consciousness, both are always in contact. They can never be separated.

Inner Voice

Listen to the self The voice within
The Ved and the Koran will always win

There are no casts In the house of the Lord
There are no sunnis Nor shias at all

There are no Brahmans No sudra are there
There are no religions Only goodness is there

Loving and caring And your body will shine
Those that forget Have a satanic mind

Look into yourself You will see your sins
You will then realise The badness within

Control the self The thoughts within
Caring actions for all Only goodness can win

Purify your soul With thoughts of love
Cleanse your mind Be one with God

Poem 34

The mind at its highest spiritual elevation is the fountain of all knowledge, it has direct contact with the Super Soul also known as Super Consciousness. We have to develop our inner intuition through worldly knowledge, meditation and righteous thoughts and deeds.

Vedas are the scriptures of Hinduism, the Koran is the holy book of the Muslims. Brahmans are the highest cast of the Hindu cast system and sudra are the lowest in the cast. There are no religions or casts in the House of God, only ultimate love and equality for all.

Those that love and care for other people, are creating a good karmic account. Those who discriminate on cast, gender, country, colour or religion can be considered to have satanic minds. If you look into your own consciousness, you will see the darkness of your own wrong deeds, the badness within. One has to take responsibility for his/her own actions.

Karma are our deeds good or bad.

Light

Love is light It shines so bright
Love is surrender Ego is not so right

Love is God In the hearts of all
Love is heaven The destination of all

Love is pure It is very very strong
It never ever dies It always goes on

It lives within Our heavenly spark
Divine Love within Is the light in the dark

Love is forgiveness All of the time
There are no conditions Love is divine

Love them all The good and the bad
Guide the lost On a righteous path

Love is light It shines so bright
Love is surrender Ego is not so right

Poem 35

Love is enlightenment, love is God. If you do not surrender you are not in love. Ego is destructive there is no room in love for ego. There is unlimited love in the hearts of all, it costs nothing to love and be nice. Divine Light of Love is our final destination.

The Kingdom of Heaven is Love. Finally we will all merge into the eternal infinite ocean of love. Love has no conditions, love is forgiveness. True Love is very strong, it is immortal.

We all must love everyone, the good and the bad and guide those that are lost on the path of righteousness.

Loving, helping, caring and sharing is a very good way of making friends and winning over people who may have misunderstandings with us. Ultimate Love is bliss.

Had To Go

When I came into this world I did not know
Why I was born And where I had to go

Life was good My mind was clean
I had some desires They were not so mean

I crossed my limits I crossed the wire
My thoughts and actions Were a selfish fire

My soul within Is torn apart
Little peace within To sooth my heart

I need no scripture I need no religion
To show me the path To my heavenly Kingdom

I need to focus On the light within
Suppress my ego And thoughts within

The Father of creation Is deep within
The love of a Guru Takes you to him

Poem 36

When I was born I had limited consciousness and understanding. My guidance help and support come from my parents and family. As I grew up I had to learn the hard way through my own experiences. I could not understand what my parents were trying to say and why. Eventually when I realised what they were saying, I still wanted to have my own way whenever I could get away with it.

As I grew up I became aware of the bright lights of the world and the pleasures of the physical body. Friends meant everything to me, ego selfishness and anger started taking over my personality.

After many slaps on my face, I realised that my shellfish attitude was not the way forward. I took trying to understand life through religion and scriptures. I came to the conclusion that love is the cream of all religions. Love comes from within, being loved leads to happiness. It does not cost anything to be nice.

The most important thing is not to have ego or anger. Focus within for wisdom, strength and guidance. Of course having a spiritual master in one's life is a catalyst to focusing on the path of righteousness.

Destination

So far in my life I have learned a little
I have worked quite hard And earned a little

One thing of importance Was the goodness I gave
I suffered a lot For the love I craved

What have I achieved In this world of madness
Is it all a dream Of happiness and sadness

I cannot ignore This dream of my life
I need to be good And always be wise

Survival is a must Health must come first
Sow good seeds For other people's needs

We all move on So prepare and be strong
Do good deeds And sow good seeds

Our ultimate goal Is to realise the self
The Inner soul Where heavenly love dwells

Poem 37

In life we need to learn and earn and be good to all. Every now and then we have to assess what we are doing, what we have achieved or what we have lost. Why we have suffered and what happiness we have got. What is relevant and what is irrelevant. This whole worldly play seems to me as a dream. But for the present moment it is a reality, I am part of this dream world reality.

The most important thing in this dream play is survival. The only thing guaranteed is death. A fact is that one day we will all move on from this dream world, into another dream. Thus we need to prepare ahead. We need to know what we have to do, where we are coming from, where we are going and how to get there.

We need righteousness and we need a spiritual guide. Our final destination is with our Heavenly Father, who loves us more than anybody in this world, all he expects is a clean heart, good deeds and love.

Forever

Into this world I came to stay
Not forever Don't get in my way

In the highest of creation I was born to live
To seek his love And surrender to his will

The body is dust The soul moves on
Our karmic actions Helps us along

The journey is tough When things go wrong
Look into yourself and Sing God's song

The message is clear Please love and serve
Help those in need And care for yourself

Evil thoughts of sin Come from within
Mislead you along Darkness wins

Never ever give in The light is within
Fight the devil For you are the king

The soul is within The father of creation
The heavenly father Of Love and salvation

Cleanse the soul and Habits within
The path of righteousness Is the only thing

When the soul is clean You can never be mean
For I and the father Are both within

Into this world I came to stay
Not for ever Don't get in my way

Poem 38

We have all evolved to the highest stage of God's creation. The nature of man is to look for eternal peace happiness and true love, which we can never find on this earthly plane. Our final abode and destination is with our heavenly father within our own consciousness. Only there we will find the happiness and bliss that we are craving for.

Negative thoughts come from our ego and greed. These thoughts can lead us into actions that sin. We must fight the devil within. We have the power to win if we keep focused on righteous karma.

Our experiences on earth and guidance from scriptures and spiritual men help us to focus on our journey to eternal happiness. We must surrender to righteous deeds prayer and meditation. Attachment to material comforts and family and friends, upsets our mental stability and focus and prevents us from moving on.

We face many problems tests and trials in this journey. Eventually we learn to surrender to his will. To survive and progress, we have to tap on our inner strength. Inner strength comes from Divine love. Nothing is more powerful than having faith on Divine Love.

The body gets recycled into the earth, the soul moves on into other dream worlds according to it's karmic account.

God the father of creation is within our consciousness. To get to him we have to go deep into our consciousness with a clean mind and righteous actions.

Tests

Life flows through Many tests and trials
My mind flies around Does'nt rest for a while

Memories of events They come and they go
Some are good Some are rotten to the toes

Imagination at times May run a riot
Judgement at times No justice but a lier

In the worldly sense It is important to know
Who is good And what trouble someone sows

Thoughts of goodness Of bliss they should be
No doubts at all Of what my mind see's

Life flows through Many tests and trials
My mind flies around Does'nt rest for a while

Poem 39

In this journey of life one goes through many temptations and wrong desires. The mind flies around from one thought to another and from one desire to another. It is never happy with what it has achieved. Our experiences of sorrow, pain, pleasure and desires manifest as thoughts to haunt us.

We are always judging other people and events. At times our imagination runs of at a tangent. We think we know it all, but we know very little. Some information we do need to know to avoid pitfalls in our own lives, and those of our family and friends and other people.

Silence is golden thoughts should be of bliss and be free from doubt. Intuition comes from focusing on facts and knowledge and intellectual judgement. Through simran one can separate rights from wrongs and interpret feelings and dreams.

Dream

The dream of this world Will fade away
The reality of consciousness Will always stay

The material world Will always change
Illusion of the mind Never remains the same

The past and the future Are all in the mind
The present is here Then vanishes in time

Goodness is great It reflects your mood
Love is an attachment For the foolish dude

Bliss is beyond The senses my friend
Divine Love is eternal It can never ever end

The dream of this world Will fade away
The reality of consciousness Will always stay

Poem 40

Life is going to fade away like a dream, but the reality of consciousness will always be around. The material world is the illusion of the mind, it is always changing.

The present vanishes into the past and the future becomes the present. Everything is always on the move.

For me the goodness I give and the goodness I get, make me feel great. Too much love for someone causes attachment, which eventually turns into sorrow as nothing is permanent. Bliss is beyond the senses of the physical body, bliss is God communion. God can never give us sorrow.

Divine

Love is divine No limits my friend
God is eternal And Satan will end

Satan is within Has anger and greed
God is love Serves every one's need

Fight your senses To control your will
Suppress your ego Be calm and still

Help and support All those in need
Always be good Never show any greed

Avoid confrontation Be sensible and wise
Never say anything To regret and say bye

Have good friends That stand by your side
Forget the others They will always bite

Love is divine No limits my friend
God is eternal And Satan will end

Poem 41

Divine Love is within our own consciousness. God is Divine Love and God is also the Super Soul. The Super Soul has no beginning and no ending. God is the creator and the controller and the power within all creation. Everything that God has made will dissolve back into God, even Satan as God has made Satan.

Satan is external and internal. Internal Satan is the part of our free will that leads us away from the path of righteousness. Godly feelings are those which reject negative thoughts and turn our attention to do good deeds. Satan is also greed and ego, it causes arguments and fights and frustration. An internal battle within our consciousness is always on the go, between goodness and our egoistic inclinations. If we can avoid arguments and confrontations then we have defeated Satan.

It is good to have friends that believe in you and stand by you. If they doubt what you say, they are not worthy of being close friends and should be kept at arm's length. You should have no doubts that you are right. You must always be good and right. But on the other hand be prepared to apologise and repent if you unknowingly happen to be wrong.

Life

Life is wonderful Live it to the full
Be happy and merry Never be a fool

Life is a challenge The high and the low
Never give in Nor go too slow

Love your friends And family that matter
Others may sink Your ship in deep waters

Time is important It never comes back
Once it is gone It never plays back

Never be sad Don't make anyone mad
Whatever you do Make everyone glad

Life is like chess And snakes and ladders
Always be careful Don't slip and splatter

Don't be emotional For your lose or gain
Everything moves on Your money and your fame

Poem 42

Life is a wonderful gift. Enjoy life within whatever restrictions are imposed on the self. We can't have everything we want. It is very important to get adjusted to what we can have and what we cannot have. Work hard have realistic aims and build up for whatever you want in life. Don't go too slow nor too fast. You may burn yourself out.

Be careful who you make your friends, not all people can be trusted, be respectful to all. Time is very important, make the most of whatever time God has blessed you with.

Always try to please other people keeping your own happiness and priorities in focus. Never get too attached to anything or anybody. Everything we have has to move on one day. When you gain something you get happiness, when you lose something it brings sorrow. Never get too emotional about loss or gain.

Mother

Mother I love you I love you so much
I am lost without you You mean so much

When things went wrong You stood by my side
You showed me the path That was always bright

Whatever I needed You did your best
With love and care You showered the rest

The body is dust To the dust it belongs
Your soul is eternal To sing God's song

Where ever I go You will always be there
Your goodness within me I will always be fair

I will always be good And never be bad
For you will be hurt It will break your heart

You live within me Your memories go on
The soul of my soul To God you belong

I pray to the Lord To look after you
With heavenly peace Be one with you

When my time is over I will have to move on
The light of your soul Will guide me along

Mother I love you I love you so much
I am lost without you You mean so much

Poem 43

The relationship between a mother and her children in the worldly sense is like God to all of creation. A mother gives her children all her love and care and brings then up the best way she knows how, within her limitations. The bond between a mother and her children is very special one, very spiritual and very strong.

No one can comfort and make one feel better than a mother. When one's mother dies, one feels as if he/she has lost everything.

Although a soul moves on according to its karmic deeds through its evolutionary journey, it remains in our memory consciousness and is always with us.

Ethics and morals and the way in which a mother brings up her children, always remain in our sub consciousness, to guide us through our journey of life.

A mother can be considered to be the soul of our soul. God is the soul of all souls. He cares for us far more than a mother can care for us, God has no worldly limitations. Only God can give us the peace harmony and bliss that we are all internally craving for.

Santa

Santa is the goodness Of Christmas my son
Santa is love For all and every one

The Santa spirit Keeps Christmas alive
Santa and Jesus Will never ever die

Santa is within All caring people
Jesus was born To get rid of evil

Be a good person The is the message of love
The son of God Divine teachings he taught

He died for our sins To forgive us all
He lives within The heaven of us all

Believe in Santa Don't ever deny him
Love them all Don't ever defy him

Santa is the goodness Of Christmas my son
Santa is love For all and everyone

Poem 44

Religious festivals help to keep religions alive. The concept of Santa is very important to keep Christianity alive. Through the concept of Santa, families come together. Children are inspired and made conscious of the ethics and morals through which mankind evolves, to his final destination with our heavenly father.

Man has to better himself in all walks of life and yet have no attachment to this worldly plane as we all have to move on one day.

The basic teaching's of all religions is love, unity, helping, caring and sharing. All these qualities are naturally inherent within all of us. Christmas and Santa, help us to bring these qualities out in ourselves.

The Self

The purpose of life Is to realise the self
The soul is immortal And pure in it self

In the body it resides But not forever
The body falls off It goes on forever

The light is within Seek it to win
Sow good seeds Of goodness to swim

Loving emotions Should always flow
Surrender to goodness Don't ever let go

Our friends and foes They all move on
Good deeds of love Can never go wrong

The purpose of life Is to realise the self
The soul is immortal And pure in it self

Poem 45

The soul with a body takes birth and gets lost in this worldly plane. Once it has taken birth it forgets the experience of being without a body. Through the senses of the body it gets attached to this earthly plane. It get's conditioned to it's good and bad habits and desires.

God does nothing without a purpose. We have all been given birth for a reason. The reason is self realisation to seek out the Kingdom of Heaven, within our own consciousness. To do this we have to let go of our outer consciousness and focus within, using meditation techniques as taught by our own spiritual master.

We cannot move forward if we have attachment with family and friends, the comforts of life and whatever we own.

Mad

Why am I mad I do not know
I have not been drinking Nor smoking any dope

Friends and foes They come and they go
The good and the bad And the very low

The face they show And the way they behave
Nothing is simple Of what they say

Who can I trust I do not know
I am very confused And I feel very low

Who will be with me When I have to go
Only the light My guru will show

The laws of nature Have total control
Good karmic deeds Must always flow

Why am I mad I do not know
I have not been drinking Nor smoking any dope

Poem 46

One has to work very hard, plan ahead and make the best of the situation he/she is in. What goes on and why it goes on, is very difficult to understand. The more we think and try to reason the more we can get confused.

Family and friends and the people around us have many colours to show. It is very difficult to find any real sincere friends. Realistically we are all on our own. We all came along and alone we shall go.

Just as the body cannot exist without the soul, the individual soul cannot exist without Divine Light. Known as the Word, which is also God. Divine Light will guide the soul to its final destination, according to its good and bad deeds.

Justify

Always justifying one's self Is not a wise thing to do
Being far to self critical Is not something one should do

To see what other people see Is not a bad thing to see
It also depends on Who sees and what they see.

Things can be so complex We cannot analyse to a tee
Why even bother When it does not matter to me.

It is not important Who judges and what they say
Only friends I will take seriously All the way

Have no expectations From people that you know
True friends are rare The rest you can let go

For harmony and peace Take no fuss give no stress
Respect everyone Not just those who think you the best

Always justifying one's self Is not a wise thing to do
Being far to self critical Is not something one should do

Poem 47

We all make mistakes to cover a mistake is not a wise thing to do. On the other hand don't be too hard on the self. Evaluation of the situation is very important.

When other people judge, they judge us from the way they see things. Reality is always far more complex. Never take their judgment seriously. At the same time don't ignore them either.

Harmony and peace are vital to lead a healthy and happy life. Be responsible and wise, nice and always try to be at your best.

Attitudes

People's attitudes Upset me no more
Hatred and badness Is a foolish man's goal

Holding a grudge No goodness it shows
Expecting importance Is not letting go

Search for my soul Is my ultimate goal
When my mind is clean The light it will show

Vairag is dispassion Only love no attachment
Ways of the world Have no more attraction

I love to search Only bliss can win
Vibrations of Aum The Word within

Forgive me my friends If I am wrong
Please let me go So I can march on

People's attitudes Upset me no more
Hatred and badness Is a foolish man's goal

Poem 48

In the spiritual sense one should not be disturbed by what people say. We should be conscious of our own actions and the effect our actions have on ourselves or others. Always be positive and nice to everyone.

The most important goal in our life is self realisation, in other words to make contact with our inner consciousness. This can only be achieved by evolving through material consciousness, letting go of ego and total self control. Good deeds of caring sharing and serving in the name of the Lord and meditation, is also very important.

We will be sucked into this journey once we realise that nothing and nobody on this earthly plane will give us the permanent satisfaction we are craving for. This journey we have to make on our own.

Aum are the initial thoughtrons of God, aum is the same as the Word as in the Bible. These spiritual thoughts condense into revelations as received by prophet's messengers and holy men. These revelations are not struck by two physical objects they are not uttered by any vocal cord. They flow from beyond the boundaries of the physical plane. They are not heard by our physical ears, only by our mind consciousness, when it is in contact with Divine Consciousness.

Flaws

There are far too many flaws
In my mind body and soul

My road to bliss Has too many holes
Goodness and compassion Only love must flow

Greed I call needs Can slow me down
My ego is strong It pulls me to the ground

My mind is weak No focus at times
It jumps around And nothing it finds

How do I light My path within
Surrender to the Lord No worldly sins

There are far too many flaws
In my mind body and soul

My road to bliss Has too many holes
Goodness and compassion Only love must flow

Poem 49

Our soul, mind and body have been contaminated with unnecessary earthly desires. We have become, very greedy and egoistic. As a result we find it very difficult to be faithful on the path of loving righteousness. We do not have the determination and dedication we need to meditate for inner strength and take control of our senses.

The only way to evolve through this dangerous jungle of confusion is to surrender to goodness. But our shellfish desires, weaknesses and ego get in our way.

Our mind body and soul must be in balance and in harmony with each other. When this happens our consciousness makes contact with the spiritual vibrations and consciousness of Aum. A spiritual resonant frequency is reached, "Nirvana".

Be Good

Be always good No hatred at all
God is wonderful To the tall and the small

In the name of the Lord Nothing to fear
The wisdom of love Should always be dear

Your vision and focus Will pull you within
Your goodness and love The light within

The high and the low The storms will go
The calm will come The path will show

No anger at all All ego will go
Light up your mind Only love will flow

Be always good No hatred at all
God is wonderful To the tall and the small

Poem 50

Don't hate anyone don't make enemies, life is too short. The sensible way forward is to love everyone. If you love everyone in the name of the Lord, there is nothing to fear. The wisdom of love cannot be challenged.

Good loving deeds prayer and meditation will suck you out of mortal consciousness, deep into Super Consciousness, the light within our consciousness.

In our mortal consciousness the mind never stays still. Experiences of the past and dreams of the future haunt us in thought form, they bring with them many storms of unhappiness and dissatisfaction and also loving memories.

Once we have connected with the Super Consciousness within, all storms of sadness will turn to happiness and bliss. All ego and anger will go and only love for all will flow.

Alone

We all came alone Alone we shall go
Peace and prosperity and harmony should flow

Unity and respect In a family should show
The only way forward Is to love and let go

We are not responsible For other people's deeds
Why be conscious Of unspiritual weeds

Forgive the people That stood on your toes
Leave them alone With the badness they sowed

The laws of nature Never ever forget
God only helps The righteous best

We all came alone Alone we shall go
Peace and prosperity and harmony should flow

Poem 51

The sole purpose of life is self realisation. We came into this world on our own we shall leave on our own. Our aim is to overcome ego, the temptations of wickedness and badness. Surrender to the path of goodness, help and serve others, without having any frustration or expectations.

We have to be caring and responsible to all. But our main responsibility is our own family, unity, harmony, peace and prosperity, to create a loving and caring environment. Realistically very difficult, but we must keep on trying. Forgive those that have hurt us or wronged us. Leave it to the laws of nature, they eventually catch up on everyone.

Tough

Life can be tough Not always fun and joy
We cannot have What our karma has destroyed

Finding a friend Is a challenge to the end
Many may come Sincerity vanishes round a bend

Family and relatives May last to the end
How we get on They test us till we bend

Concern they show Their acting is good
Genuine are those Who help other dudes

The laws of nature Will test us to the end
Each and everyone Has his karma to defend

What you sow So you shall reap
Egoistic habits and Righteous good deeds

Life can be tough Not always fun and joy
We cannot have What our karma has destroyed

Poem 52

We all go through many emotions of pain pleasure and sorrow in our lives. Each situation in life comes to us according to our past and present karmic deeds and the karmic deeds of the people around us. In some situations we have very little, or no control at all. To achieve our goal, faith and hard work is a must.

Trustworthy sincere friends and family are very difficult to find. Hardly anybody stands by you when you are in trouble. Your so called friends may agree you are innocent. But supporting you openly is only what a real friend, a righteous person would do. It is extremely difficult to find one.

Family may be with you to the end, but their sincerity can challenge you until you break your back. Most are very good at acting and showing concern.

Those that believe in you and stand by you in terms of righteousness are your true friends. The laws of nature are putting us to the test all the time. We all have our own actions of goodness and badness to defend.

Eat

The mind and the body Reflect what we eat
Our thoughts and karma And what we reap

A balance of fruit And veg is good
Why take a life When there is plenty of food

The nature of man Is not to hurt
To take a life Is something worse

Remember my friends The laws of nature
They never forgive A life taker

So don't forget God love's us all
All of creation Animals tall and small

The mind and the body Reflect what we eat
Our thoughts and karma And what we reap

Poem 53

God has created man as the King of this world and given him plenty of responsibility. Intelligence and power he has, to have control according to his ability. Total control lies with God.

The nature of man is to do good. Killing and hurting anyone including animals is not what God expects from us on the path of righteousness. Everything made, has been made for a purpose. The laws of nature have the power of justice.

There is no need for man to kill for food. God has supplied him with plenty of fruits, vegetables and gains to evolve on. We should not forget that God loves and cares for everything and everyone in creation, even animals.

Illusion

The world is an illusion In the mind it is
Nothing remains the same On the move it is

The present moves on And the future is born
The reality of creation Sings a new song

Where are the ones We loved so dear
They live in our hearts Never have any fear

Why the duality In all of creation
Happiness and sadness A dream of this ocean

Some are born rich And some very poor
Life is very precious We love it so dear

What is fate And who has control
The reality of nature Has righteous goals

Why do we fight And blame one another
The nature of man Has satanic colours

Poem 54

All our experiences of the people we have interacted with and whatever we have seen and heard throughout our life(s) are recorded in our dream world of consciousness. They rest deep in our sub consciousness, until something triggers them off and brings them to our attention. Everything is always on the move and can change from one extreme to the other, duality.

This moment of the present is not a dream. It is a reality that we cannot ignore. We have to monitor the dream of our past experiences and the present situation. Sow necessary seeds by karmic action, so we can have control over the dream of our future.

Without scriptures or a spiritual master we cannot understand, why one person is born in a rich family and another in a poor one. Why do some people starve or die of a sickness and other people who are perfectly healthy also die.

We fight and blame each other. Greed and ego have no satanic limits. Why can't we just enjoy life, be happy and live and let live. If we could do this, nature would have no purpose for evolution.

Special Thanks

There are many individuals who have assisted, inspired and encouraged me throughout my journey of life.

To mention a few:

Samrat Tawde Dental Surgeon – Intelligent and ambitious spiritual and down to earth for his contribution on Sanatan Dharam Chaupal Awaz FM and as a very close friend.

Supraneeti Hammacott – Talent, beauty actor and singer. Spiritual enlightenment and worldly wise. Supporting me in all walks of life especially for her contribution and support on Sanatan Dharam Chaupal Awaz FM.

Ian Stewart General Secretary Edinburgh Interfaith – Truely a great man working very hard to break down dogmatic religious barriers and boundaries.

Ann Breslin (Glasgow Peace Federation) – A remarkable women working very hard to promote 'One human family under God'. Shuba Iyer excellent personality true to herself and others.

Hunter High East Kilbride Head of Design and Technology Paul Lemon and senior teacher John Russell.

St Andrews and St Brides East Kilbride – Jerry Colgan Assistant Head Teacher and Jerry Hasset Head of Design and Technology and all staff.

Calderglen High School – East Kilbride

All staff and pupils especially all staff and technicians in the department of Design and Technology.

Mubashir Shehzad – Poet and Presenter on AwazFM and All the Management and Presenters on Awaz FM

Indian Workers Association for their passion and concern for India. Unity peace prosperity equality and harmony for everyone all over the world is their goal.

An Extra Special Thanks to Paramjit Singh Basi President of IWA Glasgow. A good friend a great man beyond the pettiness of petty politics.

Ashwin

Aswhin is the second Prince of the Nahar throne
He is very handsome Does not like to be on his own

He likes to see his cartoons He bits like a bee
If Aryan ever annoys him He fights on his knees

A cheeky little brat He can sometimes be
Nothing ever stop him With granny he wants to be

His parents have high hopes To university he will go
Will he become a doctor Or an actor in a show

Earn a lot of money And marry a beautiful lady
She has to be very special And not be very shady

Ashwin will be spiritual A yogi he will be
Walk the path of righteousness Divine light he will see

Baba Taresh
Happy 1st Birthday 27th Jan 2015

Printed in the United States
By Bookmasters